SWING KINGS

SWING KINGS

Julie Koerner

FRIEDMAN/FAIRFAX
PUBLISHERS

A FRIEDMAN/FAIRFAX BOOK

©1994, 1997 Michael Friedman Publishing Group, Inc.

Library of Congress Cataloging-in-Publication number 95-131047

ISBN 1-56799-358-3

Editor: Benjamin Boyington
Art Director: Jeff Batzli
Designer: Lynne Yeamans
Photography Editor: Jennifer Crowe McMichael

Color separations by Ocean Graphic International Company Ltd.
Printed in Singapore by KHL Printing Co. Pte Ltd.

10 9 8 7 6 5 4 3 2 1

For bulk purchases and special sales, please contact:
Friedman/Fairfax Publishers
Attention: Sales Department
15 West 26th Street
New York, NY 10010
(212) 685-6610 FAX (212) 685-1307

Visit our website: http://www.metrobooks.com

For my children, Matt and Jenna.

I would like to thank Ben Boyington for his invaluable editorial assistance.

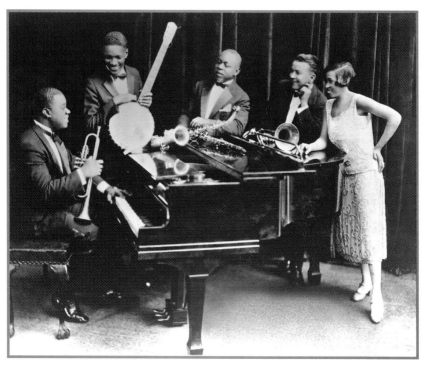

Pianist Lil Hardin, shown here with Louis Armstrong's Hot Five around 1927, was also Armstrong's wife.

Contents

The Birth of Swing

"It don't mean a thing if it ain't got that swing"

    —Duke Ellington

These words exemplify an era and an attitude, a period in history when people were

beginning to look for forms of entertainment that were both enlightening and engag-

ing. Millions found what they were looking for in a phenomenon that rose out of the

evolution of jazz: a time, a demeanor, and an era known as Swing.

    Many American cities claim to be the birthplace of jazz, but New Orleans,

whose citizens' ancestors are French, Spanish, Italian, English, German, Slavic, Creole,

and African American, may have the greatest right to that title. During the late 1800s,

when musical innovation and improvisation became the rage in New Orleans, the city's

New Orleans pianist Ferdinand Joseph La Menthe, better known as Jelly Roll Morton, in Chicago, 1924.

ize this improvisational blend of music, and is therefore regarded by many scholars, as he regarded himself (he claimed to have "invented jazz in 1902"), the father of jazz.

From its beginnings, jazz took on many different characteristics as musicians carried it through the South in the early 1900s, usually with five- or six-man bands as its vehicle. Bandleader W.C. Handy is regarded as one of the most impor-

sounds quickly spread to Memphis, Kansas City, and St. Louis. European classical, West African tribal, early gospel, and American folk intertwined to transform ragtime, the popular music of the day, into the spontaneous style of improvisation first known as "jass." New Orleans pianist Jelly Roll Morton was the first musician to popular-

W.C. Handy (1873–1958)

Born in Alabama, W.C. Handy played cornet and traveled throughout the country with many bands. He is best remembered, however, as a songwriter, and is often thought to be the first person to commit blues arrangements to paper. Some of his compositions include "The Memphis Blues," "The Joe Turner Blues," and "Beale Street Blues," all composed between 1910 and 1917. His song "St. Louis Blues" is one of the most recorded songs in music history.

Ragtime

Before the jazz outburst in New Orleans, there was ragtime, a form of composed music that was performed mostly on piano. This musical form spread through the country primarily via railroad construction teams out of Sedalia, Missouri, where Scott Joplin (1868–1917) lived and wrote ragtime songs for the piano. Ragtime music was also played on the banjo or by brass bands, but it is the piano compositions that have stayed with us; the most well-known of these are the Joplin songs "The Entertainer," which became famous outside musical circles around 1973, when it was used as the theme song for the

Scott Joplin's "Crush Collision March" (1896) exemplified railroad folklore.

movie *The Sting*, and "Maple Leaf Rag," which was first published in 1899.

tant early composers and documentors of the blues; two of his most important songs were "Memphis Blues" and "St. Louis Blues," written in 1912 and 1914, respectively. And in New Orleans, Dixieland music became so prevalent that bands would march in paradelike fashion down the streets; if two Dixieland bands met face-to-face, a spontaneous "battle of the bands" would ensue, to the enjoyment and delight of merchants and onlookers. Back then, bands were either all-black or all-white,

resulting in differing styles. While the white bands may have been technically precise, many of the black bands were looser, more improvisational, and more creative. It wasn't until several years later, when musicians began to choose their bandmates, rather than have them determined by social edict, that jazz as a musical form began to come of age.

In the early 1900s, jazz bands began taking their music eastward and northward, to Chicago and San Francisco. A five-member,

Dixieland

In 1919, the Jack "Papa" Laine Jazz Band, shown here at the Open-Air Theatre in Alexandria, Louisiana, made a hit of Scott Joplin's "Shadow Rag."

Dixieland music was characteristically played only by white musicians. According to many scholars, the first band to play ragtime music was formed by a drummer and alto horn player named Jack "Papa" Laine (1873–1966) in 1888. Although Laine's music became influential to the white bands that followed him, including the Original Dixieland Jazz Band (ODJB), Laine at first imitated the black bands and their music, including that of Scott Joplin. Before World War I Laine formed the Reliance Brass Band, which included Joseph "Sharkey" Bonano and Nick La Rocca, who went on to form the ODJB.

Jelly Roll Morton (1885–1941)

While jazz bands were marching along the streets of New Orleans and other American cities, the one musician not included—because of the unwieldiness of his instrument—was the pianist. Instead, ragtime and jazz pianists played their music in the saloons and brothels, and every bar and cabaret had a house pianist. This was the venue for Jelly Roll Morton and his compositions.

Often bragging that he invented jazz, Jelly Roll was a flamboyant, arrogant young man of Creole descent (his real name was Ferdinand Joseph La Menthe) who showed off his wealth by having a diamond implanted in a front tooth, and frequently complained that other musicians not only made his songs famous, but also made more money from them than he did. In the early to mid-1920s, Morton formed the Red Hot Peppers, with whom he made many recordings between 1926 and 1930, his most prolific period. One of his songs, "Tiger Rag," which was written in 1917 and recorded soon after by the Original Dixieland Jazz Band, became such a favorite that it was recorded, sometimes with a varied arrangement, by Duke Ellington, Louis Armstrong, Art Tatum, Benny Goodman, Glenn Miller, and Tommy Dorsey.

Jelly Roll Morton's Red Hot Peppers, with Kid Ory on trombone and Morton at the piano, around 1926.

King Oliver (back row, left, with trumpet) with Lil Hardin and Oliver's own Creole Jazz Band in Chicago, 1923.

jazz activity throughout the 1920s. Jelly Roll Morton transported the Red Hot Peppers. Louis Armstrong formed his famous first bands, the Hot Five and Hot Seven. And a New Orleans cornet player named Joseph Oliver (1885–1938), whom the early

all-white Dixieland band called the Original Dixieland Jazz Band became the first jazz band to make records. In 1917, the ODJB, as this band was popularly known, first played their music in New York City.

When the United States entered World War I and the port city of New Orleans was swamped by servicemen, many of the popular bands moved to Chicago, which became the epicenter of

bandleader Kid Ory—considered by many to be the first king of New Orleans jazz—nicknamed "King" of the cornet, moved to Chicago with the Creole Jazz Band. This band featured Johnny Dodds (1892–1940) on clarinet, his brother Baby Dodds (1898–1959) on drums, Honore Dutrey (1890–1937) on trombone, Lillian Hardin (1903–1971) on piano, Bill Johnson on clarinet, and Oliver on cornet. Once he added trumpeter Louis Armstrong to his band, King Oliver became known as the "King of Chicago jazz."

Louis Armstrong and King Oliver had played together for Kid Ory, who had discovered "Satchmo," as Armstrong was known, back on the streets of New Orleans. In fact, Armstrong didn't move to Chicago until Oliver sent for him in 1922. With Armstrong, Oliver's band was the hottest Chicago jazz band until Satchmo left it in 1924 to join Fletcher Henderson (1898–1952). Henderson's combo was the house band at the Roseland Ballroom in New York City, and, together with Armstrong, Coleman Hawkins, and Don Redman (1900–1964), they brought the house down nightly. Henderson's greatest strength lay in locating, recognizing, and showcasing talent. He featured solos by

The Original Dixieland Jazz Band

On a fateful day in 1917, the Original Dixieland Jazz Band played at Reisenweber's Restaurant in New York City; from that moment on they were a success.

Formed and led by cornet player Nick La Rocca (1899–1961), ODJB has come to be known as the first white jazz band. Before they disbanded, the group recorded several songs, including "Tiger Rag," "Original Dixieland One-Step," and "At the Jazz Band Ball." The popularity achieved by this band paved the way for an upsurge in jazz band appreciation, as theaters and dance halls began to fill with enthusiastic dancers and fans.

The ODJB featured (left to right) Tony Spargo, Eddie Edwards, leader Nick La Rocca, Larry Shields, and Henry Ragas.

Kid Ory (1886–1973)

Often remembered as the man who gave Louis Armstrong his first job, Kid Ory was once considered the greatest trombonist in New Orleans. Edward "Kid" Ory was born in La Place, Louisiana, and organized his first band while he was still a child. By 1911, he had formed his own band in New Orleans, which at different times featured King Oliver, Louis Armstrong, Johnny Dodds, and Jimmie Noone. By 1919, Ory had taken the band to California, calling it Kid Ory's Sunshine Orchestra, and had had the distinction of being the first New Orleans black band to make recordings. Ory moved to Chicago in the mid-1920s and was featured on Louis Armstrong's Hot Five and Hot Seven recordings, and with Jelly Roll Morton's Red Hot Peppers. Frequently moving to warmer climates for health reasons, Ory continued to rekindle and revive the New Orleans sound through the beginning of the 1970s.

Kid Ory had a part in the 1956 movie The Benny Goodman Story.

Don Redman and Benny Carter (b. 1907) on alto saxophones, and Coleman Hawkins and Leon "Chu" Berry (1910–1941) on tenor saxophones.

It was around this time that Henderson began to experiment with meter, arranging pieces in 4/4 time instead of the usual 2/4. Armstrong began to perfect these changes in his improvised solos. And as arranger, Redman began to write music that achieved a dramatic interplay between ensemble players and soloists. For instance, the music would shift up or down an octave, or soloists or solo sections would jump in unexpectedly. The music was beginning to "swing."

Fletcher Henderson is often credited with introducing Swing into jazz. Despite this, and despite Armstrong's success with Henderson, in 1924, at the height of Henderson's popularity at Roseland, Louis Armstrong departed to form his own band called the Hot Five (later the Hot Seven)—which included Kid Ory—and begin his recording career. Soon after Louis Armstrong left, Fletcher Henderson's band began to falter, not because of Henderson's inability to arrange songs or identify talent, but because of his shortcomings as a bandleader and business manager.

Once Satchmo took control of his own band, the transformations he wrought changed the course of jazz history. The shift in rhythm, the "swing" in Armstrong's

In 1924, the Fletcher Henderson Orchestra included Coleman Hawkins (left), Louis Armstrong (second from left), Fletcher Henderson (fourth from left), and Don Redman (far right).

Don Redman (1900–1964)

By the time he had reached the age of three, Don Redman had already begun to play the trumpet, and by six he had joined his first band. A prodigy, Redman could play most instruments by the time he reached adulthood. He joined Fletcher Henderson's band and recorded with Henderson before he became the musical director of McKinney's Cotton Pickers from 1927 through 1931, when he left to form his own band. Together with trumpet player and arranger John Nesbitt (1900–1935), Don Redman brought

McKinney's Cotton Pickers widespread attention and popularity by the end of the 1920s. An outstanding saxophone player, Redman is best remembered as one of the first great jazz composers and arrangers. Among many others, Redman recorded with Bessie Smith and Louis Armstrong; in the 1950s, he was musical director for Pearl Bailey (1918–1990).

Don Redman with his fifteen-member orchestra in 1934.

Louis Armstrong's first recording as a band-leader was "My Heart," in November 1925.

commercial success—and all the while, his musical sophistication was always one beat ahead of his audience. Many students of music consider Louis Armstrong the greatest soloist ever to perform; all agree that he was one of the greatest hornplayers.

By 1928, many bands, following in Armstrong's musical footsteps, had begun to play in 4/4 time, and popular jazz became synonymous with Swing. From Chicago to Kansas City to Harlem, jazz bands grew in size and in popularity, and the 1930s heralded what was to be jazz's most commercial period—the Swing era.

The beginnings of the Swing era nurtured the development of big bands. Instead of one musician per instrument, there were now several, resulting in instrumental sections: trombones, trumpets, and saxes (including tenor, alto, and perhaps soprano or baritone varieties). Bandleader Don Redman is thought by some scholars to have assembled one of

phrasing, either with his cornet or his singing voice, added Swing to jazz forever. Armstrong's innovations led to the strength and popularity of the solo within the band, and his creativity led him to great

At the same time that the big bands were touring the country, playing ballrooms and dance halls in cities across the nation, there existed another type of band whose geographical and economic limitations held their public exposure in check—territory bands, so named because restrictions prevented them from traveling outside their immediate territory. Though there is little recorded evidence of their existence, these bands made major contributions to the music world in the form of talent that found its way out of the territory covered by riverboats, carnivals, and traveling minstrel shows. One of the larger cities to spawn territory bands was Kansas City, and it is from here that Count Basie signed up with Walter Page's Blue Devils, then joined Bennie Moten's band. Noteworthy territory bands include the Ross De Luxe Syncopators, from the deep South; Jimmy Gunn's Dixie Serenaders, from Charlotte, North Carolina; the Carolina Cotton Pickers, from Birmingham, Alabama; and Sonny Clay's Plantation Orchestra and Curtis Mosby and his Dixieland Blue Blowers, from the West Coast.

the first "big bands" in 1931: a group that included three trumpets, three trombones, four saxophones, and a rhythm section consisting of piano, guitar, bass, and drums. Many of the newer orchestras restyled the traditional New Orleans–type band by replacing the tuba with the smoother, more sophisticated sounds of the string bass and the banjo with the more versatile guitar.

Swing and the Public

As the number of bands increased across the nation, public interest in listening and dancing to the music likewise increased; and as interest rose, the number of places to dance to, watch, and listen to jazz also rapidly increased. Some venues, such as the Savoy in Chicago, the Arcadia in Los Angeles, the Roseland in New York, and the Glen Island Casino outside New York City in New Rochelle, were huge ballrooms designed specifically to provide a place for the public to dance to big band music. To meet the popular demand, major hotels such as the Ambassador in Los Angeles, the Mark Hopkins in San Francisco, and the Biltmore in New York City opened up their ballrooms for the same purpose, often including dinner in the price of an evening of dancing. People who didn't live near the entertainment centers could buy records produced by Columbia and Victor and play them at home on their phonographs. Or they could listen to regular broadcasts over the radio, straight from those magical ballrooms in New York City or Chicago. Many musicians, including Benny Goodman, Glenn Miller, and Frankie Trumbauer, at one time earned their living by day as studio musicians, recording with various bands, but spent their evenings playing and improvising in nightclubs like the Cotton Club.

By the mid-1930s, thanks in large part to the transported English dancing couple Vernon (1887–1918) and Irene Castle (1893–1969), whose easy-looking sophisticated dance style caught the attention of the American dance audience, ballroom dancing had moved from private organizations and clubs into public rooms and dance halls. By the time Prohibition

The Gus Arnheim Orchestra, featuring Bing Crosby and the Rhythm Boys, pose at the Ambassador Hotel's Coconut Grove in 1930.

Swing Today

Swing music and dance is alive and well in our major cities. Today, New Yorkers interested in dancing to swing music can tap into related activities with a telephone call to the New York Swing Dance Society. Since the mid-1980s, millions of people have again been enjoying this kind of dancing, thanks to composers like Michael Feinstein and performers such as Harry Connick, Jr., whose talents have contributed to a resurgence of interest in big band music and dance. Swing dancers gather at the Rainbow Room or the Continental Club in New York and at Bentley's in San Francisco to dance to the music of Vince Giordano and the Nighthawks, the Hightops, or Don Batcho and the 2002 Orchestra. There are dance studios, such as Dance Manhattan in New York, headed by Teddy Kern, where people can learn to dance either professionally or socially, and the Sandra Cameron Studio, where students can learn from Frankie Manning, one of the remaining participants of the romantic era of Swing.

was officially brought to an end in late 1933, there were many clubs, ballrooms, and dance halls across the nation—so many, in fact, that the larger ballrooms began to compete for listening and dancing audiences by holding battles of the bands, providing a forum for bands to showcase their talents while at the same time providing nonstop music for the dancing audiences.

Trade newspapers and magazines, such as *Billboard*, *Metronome*, and *Down Beat*, provided fans with regular updates of record sales and available new recordings, music reviews, and sometimes even gossip. *Billboard*'s "Orchestra Routes" and a *Down Beat* column entitled "Where the Bands are Playing" informed people where they could watch or listen to their favorite bands. *Esquire*, *Playboy*, *Metronome*, and *Down Beat* also conducted readers' and critics' polls, bestowing accolades in categories such as favorite soloist and favorite band. Some of the larger ballrooms, such as the Hollywood Palladium and the Trianon Ballroom in Chicago, published their own newsletters. And press agents busied themselves attracting attention to their clients by publishing eye-catching or provocative press releases.

The trade magazines also published lists of top-selling records. A July 1940 *Billboard* "hit" list reads as follows:

1. I'll Never Smile Again, *Tommy Dorsey*
2. The Breeze and I, *Jimmy Dorsey*
3. Imagination, *Glenn Miller*
4. Playmates, *Kay Kyser*
5. Fools Rush In, *Glenn Miller*
6. Where Was I?, *Charlie Barnet*
7. Pennsylvania 6-5000, *Glenn Miller*
8. Imagination, *Tommy Dorsey*
9. Sierra Sue, *Bing Crosby*
10. Make Believe Island, *Mitchell Ayres*

The Bandleaders

The characterization "Swing Kings" can be interpreted in various ways. Some scholars refer to Louis Armstrong (1900–1971), whose music and style influenced virtually every diligent musician, as the first King of Swing, since he was the first to play in 4/4 time. Yet we could easily remember every bandleader of this explosive decade as a Swing King, because each was an important representative of the Swing era. By the middle of the 1930s, when Swing was filling theaters and dance halls across the country, Benny Goodman was also moving across the country, and at the end of his tour, he suddenly became the undisputed King of Swing.

Benny Goodman (1909–1986)

Benny Goodman learned to play the clarinet while still a boy, and first appeared onstage at the age of twelve with Benny Meroff in Chicago. In 1926, drummer and bandleader Ben Pollack, who had seen Goodman play in Chicago, sent for him to play the Venice Ballroom in Los Angeles. Goodman went with Pollack to New York, where for several years he played in theater orchestras, on radio programs, and for recording sessions. During this time, he met record producer John Hammond (1910–1987), who was to play a major role in

Goodman's career (and his personal life, as well, in that Goodman later married Hammond's sister). Persuaded by Hammond, Goodman hired pianist Teddy Wilson and vibraphonist Lionel Hampton to play in his newly formed combo, thus breaking ground by featuring black and white musicians playing together. In the mid-thirties, Goodman's combo played regularly for the National Biscuit Company's radio program *Let's Dance*. John Hammond also suggested to Goodman that he might be interested in using some of Fletcher Henderson's musical arrangements. Henderson, whose band had enjoyed several years in the limelight, was now struggling to keep it together, so when Benny called, a partnership was created.

Goodman took his band across the country, playing venues in major cities, but failed to attract special notice. When he arrived at the Palomar Ballroom in Los Angeles on August 21, 1935, Goodman, feeling frustrated by ambiguous audience response, decided to play his and Henderson's favorites, not the "sweet"

Benny Goodman in a promotional photograph taken in a CBS recording studio.

tunes that topped the charts. The result was incredible—the audience was spellbound. The sensational opening at the Palomar was the beginning of skyrocketing success for the Goodman band, and some historians say it marked the beginning of the Swing era. Everyone began referring to Benny Goodman as the "King of Swing."

Members of the Goodman band at times included drummer Gene Krupa, trombonist Murray McEachern (1915–1982), tenor saxophonist Vido Musso (1913–1982), vocalist Helen Forrest (b. 1918), and trumpeters Harry James, Chris Griffin (b. 1915), and Ziggy Elman (1914–1968). Some of their biggest hits were "King Porter Stomp," "Blue Skies," and "Between the Devil and the Deep Blue Sea." Within the orchestra of his big band, Goodman regularly featured solos by a quartet that included himself, Teddy Wilson, Lionel Hampton, and drummer Buddy Rich (1917–1987). Benny Goodman neither invented nor perfected the transition to Swing, but his technical expertise, business savvy, and musical virtuosity made his the most commercial band and Swing the

In 1935, Benny Goodman (right) made history when he created the first integrated professional band by featuring pianist Teddy Wilson (left) in his trio.

leading popular musical style, not just on records and in the dance halls, but with another major, so-far untapped market—college students. Accelerated recording activity, revived post-Depression interest in social entertainment, and the enthusiasm of the younger generation all contributed to make the Swing era, which extended from the early 1930s through the middle of the 1940s, the most commercially successful period in the history of jazz.

Duke Ellington (1899-1974)

Without question, one of the world's most popular and prolific musical performers and composers was Edward Kennedy Ellington, known as "Duke." From the onset of his career in the early 1920s until his death, Ellington wrote more than one thousand musical pieces. Born into a middle-class family, Duke was taught piano at an early age. With a group that came to be called the Washingtonians and included reed player Otto Hardwicke (1904–1970), drummer Sonny Greer (1903–1982), banjo player Elmer Snowden (1900–

The great Duke Ellington, shown here in the early 1930s in typically dapper fashion, not only acquired popular success, but also received critical acclaim for his music.

1973), and trumpeter Arthur Whetsol (1905–1940), Ellington's first real job was to play backup for singer Ada "Bricktop" Smith in Harlem. Soon after, the band moved to the Hollywood Club, also in New York, and added the talents of trombonist Charlie Irvis (1899–1939) and trumpeter Bubber Miley (1903–1932). At this time, Duke also began to arrange and compose in his own stylings, capitalizing on the strengths of his fellow musicians. Toward the end of 1927, Ellington moved to the Cotton Club in Harlem to become the house bandleader, where he enjoyed artistic freedom and musical success for several years, producing intricate, elaborate floor shows to accompany what some people deprecatingly referred to as "jungle music." By 1932, Ellington had a fourteen-piece band and a singer, and he and his arrangers had produced songs that exemplified the times, such as "Caravan," "Perdido," and the song that summed up the times, both socially and musically, "It Don't Mean a Thing If It Ain't Got That Swing."

At the height of success, both for his kind of music and his style of big band, Duke Ellington took his band to Europe, where he enjoyed a popularity that would not have come so readily to a black band

Jazz in Europe

During the 1930s, many American orchestras and bands were invited to tour Europe, where audiences always showed an interest in and appreciation for jazz. In 1933, the Duke Ellington Orchestra toured Europe, even performing for royalty. In fact, while Benny Goodman and Glenn Miller were enjoying their peak commercial success in the United States, Ellington remained abroad, where he enjoyed more personal and artistic freedom than he had at home. In 1934, after he left Fletcher Henderson's band, Coleman Hawkins went to England and played with bands there for several years; and although he returned to the States, he continued to tour Europe throughout the 1950s. Kid Ory toured Europe several times in the 1950s. Count Basie made his first European tour in 1954, and in 1957 his was the first American band to play a Royal Command performance for the Queen of England. During World War II and until his disappearance, Glenn Miller organized an orchestra for the American Armed Forces; this group played in England in 1944 and was broadcast to all the armed forces.

in the United States in 1933. While Ellington could and did always enjoy commercial success, it is generally agreed that he was not motivated entirely by commercial considerations—his motivation was based in his musical creativity. By 1939, Ellington had hired arranger Billy Strayhorn (1915–1967), beginning a life-long partnership that resulted in the creation of the band's theme song, "Take the A Train," and many other hits. Duke Ellington continued to tour the United States, Europe, and Africa until the late 1960s; his death (of cancer) was mourned by fans throughout the world as the loss of one of the most remarkable musical talents in history.

Count Basie (1904-1984)

Because he himself was as warm and likable as his music, William "Count" Basie brought a consistent tone to the Swing era. After being taught to play piano by his mother, the teenage Basie played piano and organ with various Harlem pianists, among them Fats Waller (1904–1943), then played the vaudeville circuit in New York City. Basie joined the Gonzel White traveling vaudeville act, which broke up in Kansas City, leaving Basie alone and stranded. After one year with Walter Page's (1900–1957) Blue Devils, Basie joined Bennie Moten's (1894–1935) band in 1929. The Moten band was popular and highly successful as it traveled throughout the country for several years, until Moten's untimely death during a tonsillectomy. This unexpected turn of events left the band with-out a leader, and, although Bennie's brother Buster tried his hand, the band eventually fell apart. Finally, Basie pulled together many of Moten's bandmembers, and Count Basie and the Barons of Rhythm were born.

Inevitably, Basie's band caught the sharp ear of producer John Hammond, who wrote glowing reviews about the band in *Down Beat* magazine, helped Basie structure recording deals, and encouraged the Count to enlarge his band, a recommendation that, by 1936, resulted in the six-teen-piece Count Basie Orchestra. The

Page, trombonists Dickie Wells (1909–1985) and Benny Morton (1907–1935), and vocalists Billie Holiday and James Rushing (1903–1972). Songs from the Orchestra during this time, such as "Jumpin' at the Woodside" and "One O'Clock Jump," became representative of the "easy" Swing of the period. Count Basie continued to form and re-form new orchestras throughout the forties, fifties, and sixties. A heart attack in 1976 slowed him down, but he continued to perform from a wheelchair until failing health finally curtailed his performing career. He died of cancer in Florida.

Orchestra enjoyed continuous success through the decade, and at times included trumpeters "Big" Ed Lewis (1909–1985) and Harry "Sweets" Edison (b. 1915), tenor saxophonist Lester Young, guitarist Freddie Green (1911–1987), bassist Walter

Lionel Hampton (b. 1913)

At the Holy Rosary Academy in Wisconsin in the early 1900s, a young man named Lionel Hampton was taught by a nun to play a simple drum. Hampton pursued his interest in percussion instruments, and by age fifteen was playing drums in local bands.

Around 1928, his family moved to Chicago, and Lionel teamed with friend Les Hite (1903–1962), who eventually formed a band that included Lionel and played at Sebastian's Cotton Club in Los Angeles. This is where Hampton met Louis Armstrong, who fronted Hite's band for the better part of a year, resulting in Armstrong inviting the entire Hite band to record with him. According to legend, Armstrong saw a set of vibraphones in a corner of a recording studio and asked Hampton to play—what a serendipitous moment!

One night at Sebastian's Cotton Club, Hampton caught the attention of Benny Goodman, and in 1936 Goodman invited Hampton to record with him, Teddy Wilson, and Gene Krupa. The quartet was so successful that Hampton continued working with Goodman until 1940, when he left to start his own band, which at times included Charles Mingus (1922–1979), Dexter Gordon (1923–1990), and Quincy Jones (b. 1933). Over the next four

Lionel Hampton's exuberance showed in all of his performances.

decades, Lionel Hampton continued to travel through the United States and Europe, entertaining an admiring public with his immeasurable flair and incomparable style. He remained active in the music business, entertaining and nurturing new talent, up until his death.

Jimmie Lunceford (1902–1947)

Jimmie Lunceford, a skilled musician and absolute perfectionist, was the leader of one of the Swing era's most popular bands. From 1937 through 1941, the Jimmie Lunceford Orchestra at times included trumpeter Sy Oliver (1910–1988), pianist Edwin Wilcox (1907–1968), trombonist Trummy Young (1912–1984), and drummer James Crawford (1910–1980).

As a boy in Denver, Lunceford acquired a love of music from his choirmaster father. He studied music at Fisk University in Nashville and subsequently began a career as a high school music teacher in Memphis. His first musical group, which featured saxophonist Willie Smith (1908–1967), pianist Edwin Wilcox (1907–1968), and trombon-

Many bandleaders of the Swing era attributed their surprising commercial success to the distinctive influences of the popular Jimmie Lunceford Orchestra, which during its heyday was one of America's favorite dance bands.

ist Henry Wells (b. 1906), was eventually hired to play at Harlem's Cotton Club. Jimmie Lunceford was a vivacious and exciting bandleader, and his was one of

America's favorite dance bands. While the band's styles often reflected the talents of Sy Oliver, arranger of many of the orchestra's musical numbers, it is another arranger, Eddie Durham (1906–1987), who is credited with many of Lunceford's hits of the Swing era, including 1939's "Lunceford Special," featuring the trumpet solo of Snookie Young, who had replaced Eddie Tompkins that same year. Jimmie Lunceford was a superior showman, and his style and perfectionism brought his band great commercial success during Swing's most popular period. Eventually, however, the difficulties of life on the road took their toll on Lunceford, and he died of a heart attack while signing autographs.

Glenn Miller (1904-1944)

One of Jimmie Lunceford's greatest fans was a trombone player from Iowa named Glenn Miller. In the early 1930s, after stints as a bandmember with Ben Pollack, Paul Ash, and Red Nichols (1905–1965), Miller

Glenn Miller's unexplained disappearance in 1944 shocked the world.

became a popular studio musician. As an arranger for the Dorsey Brothers, and later for Ray Noble, Miller began to develop a style called "reed section voicing," that is, permitting the clarinet to dominate the saxophones. Around 1938, the Glenn Miller Orchestra enjoyed the height of its commercial success with its hits "In the Mood," "Little Brown Jug," and "Moonlight Serenade," which became the band's theme song. In 1942, the patriotic Glenn Miller joined the army and formed a large orchestra that played throughout Europe until his plane disappeared during a flight from England to France in 1944. The plane—and Miller's body—was never found.

Woody Herman (1913-1987)

Woody Herman was born in Milwaukee and began his musical career playing clarinet and alto saxophone with the Isham Jones band. When Jones broke up the band, Woody formed a group he called "the band that plays the blues" and recorded the Joe Bishop composition "Woodchopper's Ball," the song that would

In the 1940s, the Woody Herman Band performed in the films **What's Cookin'** *with the Andrews Sisters and* **Summer Holiday** *with Sonja Henie.*

songs that became instant hits with the dancing public as well as with college students, making Woody Herman one of the top bandleaders of the mid-forties. Then, to everyone's dismay, he announced he was quitting the business to spend more time with his family. But after working as a disc jockey, he became restless and formed another group, appropriately called the Second Herd, which included Stan Getz (1927–1991) and Zoot Sims (1925–1985). In 1949, after more changes in the band's roster, the group became known as the Third Herd. Herman continued to play and record with various musicians into the early 1980s, when he opened a short-lived jazz club in New Orleans.

Teddy Wilson (1912-1986)

The son of two schoolteachers, Teddy Wilson studied music in college and was an accomplished pianist and violinist, but he did not achieve national fame until he joined the Benny Goodman Trio, breaking the racial barrier in American music. Before joining the Goodman Orchestra, Wilson

remain Herman's theme song throughout his lengthy career. When World War II broke out and many musicians enlisted or were drafted, Herman formed a group that was dubbed Herman's Herd, later referred to as his First Herd, which produced many

played with Louis Armstrong, Jimmie Noone (1895–1944), and Benny Carter, with whom he was recording when he caught the attention of legendary producer John Hammond. Wilson performed with the Goodman band until he formed his own band in 1939, for which he composed or arranged much of the music. After this band's short-lived success, which included many of Billie Holiday's most outstanding performances, Wilson continued to play frequently with Goodman and other bands, then followed the path his parents had carved for him and became a music teacher, both privately and at Juilliard, for several years. He died in Connecticut.

The Dorsey Brothers

Jimmy (1904–1957) and Tommy (1905–1956) Dorsey were brothers whose musical careers ran a close parallel for many years until a personality clash sent them their separate ways. They learned to play while still children; Jimmy learned to play the clarinet and alto saxophone, and Tommy picked up the trombone and trumpet. As young men, they played as studio and recording musicians with Jean Goldkette (1899–1962) and Paul Whiteman, until they formed the Dorsey Brothers in 1929 and recorded a song that would remain Tommy's theme, "I'm Getting

In 1940, Teddy Wilson disbanded his orchestra and formed a sextet.

Opposite: Jimmy (left) and Tommy Dorsey (right), shown here in 1934, split the following year in a violent onstage breakup.

Sentimental Over You." The Dorseys' band, which included Glenn Miller, went on under Jimmy's auspices after the brothers had an onstage fracas and Tommy left to start his own (successful) band, which included singers Jo Stafford and an eager young vocalist named Frank Sinatra (b. 1915). The brothers reunited in 1953 and formed the Dorsey Brothers Orchestra. In 1955, they had their own television show for CBS, called *Stage Show.* They were still recording and playing together at the time of Tommy's death at his Connecticut home the following year. Jimmy tried to keep the band together by himself until illness forced him to retire in 1957.

Artie Shaw (b. 1910)

In 1935, Artie Shaw performed a composition of his own in which he featured a string quartet. The presence of the string section, even though it had previously been experimented with by Benny Goodman, raised a

Artie Shaw, shown here in a publicity still, was one of the first bandleaders to organize USO entertainment during World War II.

controversy that attracted great attention to Shaw's band, but by 1936 this attention had flagged. Shaw's next venture was called "Artie Shaw and His New Music," but Shaw changed his music and his band eight times between 1936 and 1955, when he formally retired. In the meantime, he honed his skills on the clarinet, and in 1939 released Cole Porter's "Begin the Beguine," which became an immediate commercial success and enabled Shaw to challenge Benny

Paul Whiteman (1890–1967)

To some, Paul Whiteman was the first "King of Jazz." To others, he was simply a sharp-eyed, well-organized bandleader. Regardless, he had an undeniable knack for spotting—and spotlighting—talent, and many musicians who went on to successful careers of their own began those careers in a Paul Whiteman band. Over the years, beginning in New York and moving west to California, Whiteman's bands included such great musicians as Jimmy and Tommy Dorsey,

Jack and Charlie Teagarden, Frankie Trumbauer, Red Norvo, Mildred Bailey, Bix Beiderbecke, Bing Crosby (1904–1977), Johnny Mercer (1909–1976), and Hoagy Carmichael (1899–1981).

The Paul Whiteman Orchestra in a publicity photograph from the 1930 film **The King of Jazz.**

Whiteman was the first bandleader of record to fully arrange his musical numbers, thereby allowing audiences to become familiar with them, which helped enhance the popularity of the music. His was the first band to feature a female vocalist (Mildred Bailey) and also the first to feature a vocal trio, called the Rhythm Boys, which included Bing Crosby, Harry Barris, and Al Rinker. A superb businessman and showman, Paul Whiteman made his mark in music history by attracting major talent and treating his musicians with respect.

Goodman in his role as "King of Swing." In 1985, Shaw came out of retirement to organize a group that would be representative of his previous Swing band.

Harry James (1916–1983)

Harry James, who had played the trumpet since he was thirteen, was twenty years old when he left Ben Pollack to join Benny Goodman's band early in 1937. Only two years later, however, James left Goodman to start his own band. James had a vibrant personality to match his sharp-toned trumpet playing, and as a bandleader was successful at creating dance music that appealed to mass audiences. Harry James appreciated vocalists, and his band characteristically featured a strong singer, such as Helen Forrest, and a young man whom James was the first to discover: Frank Sinatra.

The Soloists

The two most outstanding characteristics to develop during the Swing era may seem a bit contradictory: the emergence of the big band and the simultaneous evolution of the solo performer within a band. Instead of being contradictory, however, they are in fact complementary: one empowered the other. Solos, most often featuring a single musician (instead of a solo section), became a way for musicians to showcase their talents and at the same time add drama to the whole arrangement. Many musicologists consider Louis Armstrong the greatest soloist of all time, although there were several others whose talent was highlighted during the 1930s.

Coleman Hawkins (1904–1969)

Coleman Hawkins was born in Missouri, played piano at a very young age, and picked up his first saxophone at age nine. By age seventeen he was playing his music in Kansas City; he soon moved to Chicago, then to Los Angeles, and finally to New York, where, in 1923, he competed for and won a position as a reed player in Fletcher Henderson's Orchestra, at the same time Louis Armstrong played with Henderson. Hawkins became famous for his melodic, romantic tenor saxophone solos, then left

In 1940, Coleman Hawkins toured with a sixteen-member band, which he soon disbanded so that he could play in combos.

"Body & Soul." Although his band never reached the height of success warranted by his individual talent, Hawkins was the predecessor of many leading tenor saxophonists.

Lester Young (1909-1959)

Born into a musical family, Lester Young spent much of his youth in New Orleans. In 1934, Young wrote to Count Basie and Bennie Moten, was invited to audition, and earned a position in the band. Because of his unique sound, which some say was the result of Young's efforts to imitate Frankie Trumbauer's C-melody saxophone, Young was often highlighted in band solos. After sitting in with the Fletcher Henderson Orchestra to fill in for Coleman Hawkins, Young was hired to

the band in 1934 to travel overseas; a vivid interest in jazz had arisen in Great Britain. Hawkins returned to the States in 1939, formed his own nine-piece band, and recorded the song that immortalized him,

replace Hawkins when the latter left for Europe. Because Young was either unable or, more likely, unwilling to abandon his own style and imitate Hawkins', his time with Henderson was short. Young continued to play with various bands, frequently returning to play with the Count Basie Band. His smooth tenor saxophone solos are sometimes referred to as the sound that inspired the transition from "hot" to "cool" jazz.

Gene Krupa (1909-1973)

Drummer Gene Krupa is most often credited with drawing attention to the musical merit of the percussion instruments. By age eleven, Krupa was performing in Chicago, where he was born, with a band called the Frivolians. He played in the pit orchestra for George Gershwin (1898–1937), and with Red Nichols and Bix Beiderbecke before his famous pairing with Benny Goodman, which had been orchestrated, not surprisingly, by John Hammond. Krupa's outstanding, often outlandish drum solos were a defining characteristic of the Goodman Orchestra, and even of the quartet within the orchestra, which included Goodman, Teddy Wilson, and Lionel Hampton. In 1938, after a public quarrel with Goodman,

Many of his peers considered Lester Young the greatest tenor saxophonist of his day.

Gene Krupa's unique style of showman-ship included gum-chewing or talking to himself—or both.

Charlie Christian (1916–1942)

Although Charlie Christian lived a short life, he managed to pack an astounding musical legacy into that tenure. Born in Dallas in 1916, Christian grew up in Oklahoma City, Oklahoma, where he learned to play the guitar. Many music scholars attribute to Christian the introduction into jazz of the electric, or amplified, guitar. Charlie Christian was "discovered" by the ubiquitous John Hammond, who persuaded Benny Goodman to listen to the guitarist. Thereafter, Christian played with the Goodman Orchestra, often with Goodman's smaller sextet. Once the Goodman band moved to New York, Christian would play into the late night with the Orchestra, then go to local jazz clubs and play on into the morning.

Krupa quit Goodman's band to form his own group, which featured singers Roy Eldridge and Anita O'Day. In 1954, Krupa and Cozy Cole opened a drum school, and Krupa continued to perform occasionally until he died of leukemia.

It was probably in these early morning hours that Christian honed an interest in what would become jazz's next phase, bebop. He died of tuberculosis in New York City.

Charlie Christian is sometimes credited with coining the word "bebop," which some say evolved from sounds he made while he hummed as he played the guitar.

Jack Teagarden (1905-1964)

Jack Teagarden has the reputation of being one of the greatest and truest blues trombonists and singers. Because he taught himself to play the trombone, he had an unusual style that actually allowed him to hold notes longer than conventionally trained trombonists. It was often said that his singing voice so closely paralleled the sounds he could create on his trombone that listening audiences could not distinguish between his horn and his voice. Growing up in Texas, Teagarden lived with his family next door to a vacant lot on which a revival tent was hastily constructed; because of this, he became familiar with blues and gospel through the spirituals he heard as a child. Teagarden worked in New York City for Ben Pollack, then joined the Paul Whiteman Band, where he remained for five years until he formed his own band. But because the Swing era was winding down, and Teagarden proved not to be terribly gifted as a businessman, his band did not last very long. Teagarden spent the thirties and for-

Jack Teagarden was featured in **Birth of the Blues** *with Bing Crosby in 1941.*

ties playing with various bands and small combos, including Louis Armstrong's All-Stars from 1947 until 1951. He died of pneumonia.

Art Tatum (1909–1956)

Art Tatum, who was nearly blind, was encouraged to study violin by his piano-playing mother and guitar-playing father. While still a teen, he switched to piano and took his formal early training to the local clubs in his hometown of Toledo, later play-ing also in Cleveland and other nearby cities. By age eighteen, he had a regular job on station WSPD in Toledo, and began to establish his reputation as an expert soloist. In 1932 he went to New York to accompany vocalist Adelaide Hall, and spent the next few years playing and recording in New York and Chicago. Most of Tatum's career was etched out as a soloist, playing at private parties and in a featured spot on *The Bing Crosby Show*; he didn't formally join a combo until 1943, when he and bassist Slam Stewart (1914–1987) and guitarist Tiny Grimes (1917–1989) formed a trio. Tatum continued to play and record into the mid-1950s, when he died of uremia.

Earl "Fatha" Hines (1903–1983)

Encouraged to play the piano and organ by his musical parents in his hometown near Pittsburgh, pianist Earl "Fatha" Hines moved to Chicago in 1924 at the encouragement of friend Eubie Blake (1883–1983) to start his first band. There he became a close friend of neighbor Louis Armstrong, and

Ben Pollack (1903–1971)

Born in Chicago, drummer Ben Pollack formed his first band in 1925 in California, and moved himself and his band around the musical centers—Chicago and New York—for over a decade. Pollack's band featured many musicians whose talents would continue to rise after their departure from his band, such as Benny Goodman, Glenn Miller, Jack and Charlie Teagarden (1913–1984), and Jimmy McPartland (1907–1991). When Pollack disbanded his group in 1934, many of the remaining bandmembers went on to fame under the auspices of the Bob Crosby orchestra. Pollack's assertive, outgoing personality combined with his ability to recognize musical talent made him a gregarious and successful bandleader.

The Ben Pollack Orchestra, featuring Jack Teagarden on trombone and Benny Goodman on clarinet, at the Park Central Hotel in New York City, in August 1929.

was a member of Armstrong's Hot Five and Hot Seven during their recording sessions in 1927 and 1928, when the famous "Weather Bird" was recorded. Considered one of the greatest pianists by many jazz enthusiasts, Hines led his own bands periodically between 1928 and 1948; these bands at times included Charlie Parker, Dizzy Gillespie (1917–1993), and a singer Hines discovered named Sarah Vaughan (1924–1990). In the fifties, Earl Hines moved to northern California, where he continued to play off and on until his death.

Red Norvo (b. 1908)

Born Kenneth Norville, Red Norvo learned to play the piano while still a child, and later learned the xylophone, joining a band called the Collegians in Chicago before finishing high school. He moved around the Midwest with various bands for several years until he joined Paul Whiteman in Chicago to record. He mar-

ried Whiteman's singer, Mildred Bailey, and the two traveled together for several years. In 1935, Norvo formed a sextet that eschewed the popular Dixieland style for a more sophisticated style of Swing, thanks in large part to the arrangements of Eddie Sauter (1914–1981). After his own band split, Norvo went on to play with Benny Goodman and Woody Herman; he some-

Frankie Trumbauer (1900–1956)

Born in Carbondale, Illinois, and raised in St. Louis, Frankie Trumbauer was playing flute, trombone, and piano while still a youth but began to shine on C-melody saxophone by seventeen, when he formed his own band. (The C-melody saxophone, often mistaken for the alto sax, is really a pitch between alto and tenor.) In the 1920s, Trumbauer played with Bix Beiderbecke, and together they recorded many jazz classics, including "Singin' the Blues," which includes one of Trumbauer's most brilliant solos. Trumbauer is widely regarded as a great influence on later saxophone players, most notably Lester Young.

Bix Beiderbecke (1903–1931)

Born in Davenport, Iowa, into a family of German descent, Bix Beiderbecke was given formal piano instruction when he was young, but rebelled early to take up the cornet. His parents wanted Leon (his given name) to play classical music, but Bix determined by age twenty that his true love was jazz.

After he was expelled from school, Bix wound up on the road, where he became familiar with the styles of music played on riverboats traveling on the Mississippi River. In 1923, he was playing with a band called the Wolverines, whose sound was similar to the then top-rated New Orleans Rhythm Kings. He met Frankie Trumbauer and performed at various times with Jean Goldkette and Paul Whiteman. Beiderbecke developed exceptional musical skill, and his cornet solos are still appreciated today. His early classical training was evident in much of his music, especially on the piano. But Beiderbecke lived as hard as he played, and he developed lung illness and an addiction to alcohol at a very early age. He died in 1931 at twenty-eight, leaving behind a musical legacy that is respected by jazz musicians worldwide.

The Wolverines, with Bix Biederbecke on cornet, in 1924.

of the bands. In 1934, Chick hired a singer named Ella Fitzgerald, and together they made many records, beginning with a hit of dubious musical merit, "A-Tisket, A-Tasket." Webb's exuberance on the drums and in his personality enabled him to enjoy success as a bandleader until his premature death of tuberculosis.

The Singers

Chicago in the 1920s also saw the rise of one of jazz's most emotional blues singers, Bessie Smith (1894–1937). In fact, in the genre that loved to assign names of royalty such as King, Duke, and Count, Bessie Smith was anointed the "Empress of the Blues." Her career began in minstrel shows and on vaudeville stages. For the four years following her recording of "Downhearted Blues," in 1923, she sang and recorded with Louis Armstrong, Fletcher Henderson, Coleman Hawkins, Don Redman, and many others.

times formed his own small combos and often joined others, and continued playing through the 1980s.

Chick Webb (1902–1939)

One of the all-time great drummers, Chick Webb was born in Baltimore; he formed his first band in 1924, with which he played many Harlem clubs. From 1933 through 1939, his was the house band at the Savoy in Harlem, and they quite frequently emerged the winner of the popular battle

Billie Holiday (1915-1959)

Following in Bessie Smith's footsteps, a singer named Eleanora McKay Holiday, known to us as Billie Holiday, became one of jazz's most sympathetic and renowned vocalists. Billie was born to unmarried teenagers, and her absentee father was a member of Fletcher Henderson's band. Barely surviving an early life that included rape, incarceration, prostitution, and alcohol and drug abuse, Billie somehow managed to catch the ear of producer John Hammond in New York in 1933, and Hammond arranged her first recording session, complete with accompaniment from the Benny Goodman Orchestra. She greatly admired the style of Louis Armstrong, and had some of her greatest successes, including 1938's "When You're Smiling," with Lester Young, who gave Billie the nickname "Lady Day." In the early 1940s, Billie wrote "God Bless the Child," a song that is as poignant and enduring today as when it was first released. Over the years, she sang with Teddy Wilson, Count Basie, Lester Young (whom she in turn nick-

Billie Holiday with the Count Basie Orchestra, with whom she frequently performed, in 1951.

named "Pres"), and Artie Shaw. As the troubles Lady Day suffered throughout her life took their toll, her soft, high-pitched voice became deeper and coarser, but always included an emotional quality that has made her unforgettable. Already a legend before her death, she suffered the ultimate indignity of being arrested on her deathbed—for narcotics possesion.

Cab Calloway (1907-1994)

Cab Calloway was both a singer and a bandleader. Working first with a band called the Alabamians, then with the Missourians, Calloway initially achieved notoriety with his recording of "Minnie the Moocher," a bit of a novelty, but a song that demonstrated his vocal ability and his penchant for scat; he eventually became known as the "hi-de-ho man." While many jazz purists discount Calloway's popular songs, claiming that they have little musical merit, Calloway nevertheless had an outstanding voice with a huge range, and he had the ability to change his vocal sound; also, he enjoyed many years of success with his band, whose arrangements were built around his singing but also provided a forum for his strong soloists, among them Chu Berry and Dizzy Gillespie. This artistic freedom, combined with Calloway's penchant for paying his bandmembers well, made him a popular bandleader to work for; understandably, he gained more loyalty from his bandmembers than some of the other leaders of the era.

Cab Calloway, shown here in the early 1940s with his orchestra, was featured in the movie **Stormy Weather,** *and played "Sportin' Life" in the European and U.S. tours of* **Porgy and Bess.**

Bob Crosby (1913–1993)

At the height of the Swing era the Bob Crosby orchestra was formed, and successfully rejuvenated the New Orleans Dixieland style that by that time was considered passé. Formed by Gil Rodin as a cooperative band—that is, a group in which the members shared in the ownership and the profits—the band was fronted by singer Bob Crosby, younger brother of the more famous Bing. Like his brother, Bob had a smooth, deep singing voice. Many of the bandmembers had come out of the Ben Pollack band when it disbanded in 1934, and Bob had been singing with Tommy Dorsey. Besides being the lead vocalist, Crosby served as the band's front man, and much of the music was arranged by bandmembers Matty Matlock, Dean Kincaide, and Bob Haggart (b. 1914). During World War II, Crosby served with the Marines; after the war, he worked in studios and on radio and television.

The Bob Crosby Orchestra, featuring the Bob Cats, sometimes performed with a caged bobcat onstage.

Anita O'Day (b. 1919)

Like that of Roy Eldridge, the career of vocalist Anita O'Day included a stint at the Three Deuces in Chicago, where she sang with the Max Miller combo in 1939. At first sounding a bit like Billie Holiday, O'Day teamed with Gene Krupa in 1941 and perfected a distinctive style for her own husky

Roy Eldridge (1911–1989)

"Let Me Off Uptown," the duet sung by Anita O'Day and Roy Eldridge, with the Gene Krupa Orchestra, was perhaps Roy Eldridge's most famous record as a singer. Although he had the talent to play several instruments, Eldridge is best known for his great trumpet style, which at times was comparable to that of Louis Armstrong. Eldridge learned to play piano at the age of six, but switched to drums and then to trumpet to play with his saxophonist brother, Joe.

Roy traveled through the country, eventually landing in New York in 1930, then went to Pittsburgh in 1933 to start a band with Joe called the Eldridge Brothers' Orchestra. After the orchestra folded, Eldridge played at times with McKinney's Cotton Pickers, Chu Berry, Teddy Hill (1909–1978), and Fletcher Henderson, alternately playing the trumpet and the flugelhorn. By the mid-thirties, Eldridge led his own band at the Three Deuces in Chicago, and in 1941 he joined the Gene Krupa Orchestra, where he probably enjoyed his greatest success as a featured soloist. During his career he toured with Benny Goodman, Count Basie, and Ella Fitzgerald, among many others, until failing health slowed him down in the 1980s.

Roy Eldridge and his band at the Three Deuces in Chicago, 1937.

voice; with Krupa, O'Day recorded many popular hits of the era, including her first recording, "Let Me Off Uptown," sung with her friend Eldridge. After leaving Krupa's band, O'Day worked for a time with

Woody Herman and with Stan Kenton (1919–1979), then rejoined Krupa from 1945 to 1946. From the 1950s on, she has continued to perform with small combos and to make public appearances.

Mildred Bailey (1907–1951)

Mildred Bailey is remembered as one of the great band vocalists of all time, and certainly as the first great white female singer (she was actually part American Indian). Bailey sang with Paul Whiteman's band from 1929 to 1936, when she and Red Norvo, whom she had met and married while both were members of Whiteman's band, left Whiteman together to front their own band, often recording songs arranged by Eddie Sauter, until 1939. Bailey was a large, flamboyant woman whose singing style was influenced by Ethel Waters (1900–1977) and Bessie Smith, yet she developed a clear, concise style of her own that carved her a permanent place in jazz history.

Below: Vocalist Anita O'Day, who could also play drums, left Gene Krupa's band to marry a golfer.

Opposite: Mildred Bailey, vocalist for Paul Whiteman and later wife of Red Norvo, in an early publicity still.

THE SINGERS ⌒ 55

teamed with Gene Krupa in 1941 and perfected a distinctive style for her own husky voice; with Krupa, O'Day recorded many popular hits of the era, including her first recording, "Let Me Off Uptown," sung with her friend Eldridge. After leaving Krupa's band, O'Day worked for a time with Woody Herman and with Stan Kenton (1919–1979), then rejoined Krupa from 1945 to 1946. From the 1950s on, she has continued to perform with small combos and to make public appearances.

Mildred Bailey (1907-1951)

Mildred Bailey is remembered as one of the great band vocalists of all time, and certainly as the first great white female singer (she was actually part American Indian). Bailey sang with Paul Whiteman's band from 1929 to 1936, when she and Red Norvo, whom she had met and married while both were members of Whiteman's band, left Whiteman together to front their own band, often recording songs arranged by Eddie Sauter, until 1939. Bailey was a large, flamboyant woman whose singing style was influenced by Ethel Waters (1900–1977) and Bessie Smith, yet she developed a clear, concise style of her own that carved her a permanent place in jazz history.

Ella Fitzgerald (1918-1996)

Ella Fitzgerald was discovered when she won first prize at amateur night at the Apollo Theatre in Harlem. She joined Chick Webb's band in 1934, and stayed with him

A publicity photograph of Ella Fitzgerald.

From 1937 until his tragic death in 1941, tenor saxophonist Chu Berry was a featured member of the Cab Calloway band.

Life on the Road

Life on the road could be strenuous and arduous, and conditions were usually less than ideal. Bands often traveled by bus, covering many miles overnight through inclement weather and over dangerous roads. Bandleader Hal Kemp (1905–1940) and tenor saxophonist Chu Berry were both killed in automobile accidents. Black bands suffered the greatest indignities because they were not allowed to stay in the better hotels or choose where they wanted to eat. Some clubs wouldn't even permit black bands to play, and members of those bands certainly were not allowed to socialize with the clientele. Needless to say, personal affronts such as these did not contribute to a band's self-esteem, or nurture its interest in pleasing white audiences or bookers. While Billie Holiday was traveling with the Artie Shaw band, she felt such discrimination as the only black member of the band that she left the group to sing on her own. It is easy to imagine that one female vocalist traveling with a band under these conditions might find the circumstances difficult to handle. Marriages and dissolutions of relationships were frequent among bandmembers who spent all of their days on the road. The stress of the hard travel often took its toll in the form of excess drinking, health problems, or conflicts between bandmembers.

The Movies

The music and dance of the Swing era became the subject of several Hollywood movies in the middle of the 1930s. *Swing Time*, produced in 1936, starred Fred Astaire and Ginger Rogers in a story about love between dance partners. The 1937 film *Swing High, Swing Low* starred Fred MacMurray and Carole Lombard as a trumpeter and the wife who saved him from self-destruction.

By the early 1940s, Hollywood had decided to capitalize on the booming business of big bands. Many musicians, undoubtedly lured by the promise of big money and fame during wartime limitations, went to Hollywood to make movies. The Glenn Miller Orchestra was featured in *Sun Valley Serenade* in 1941 and *Orchestra Wives* in 1942. A 1948 movie entitled *A Song Is Born* is worth watching to see Louis Armstrong, Charlie Barnet, Benny Goodman, Lionel Hampton, and Tommy Dorsey. Tommy and his brother, Jimmy, starred in a 1947 movie about themselves entitled *The Fabulous Dorseys*. The 1953 movie *Stage Door Canteen*, about entertaining the armed forces during World War II, features the bands of Benny Goodman, Count Basie, Xavier Cugat (1900–1990), Guy Lombardo (1902–1977), and Kay Kyser (1906–1985). The real

Jack Webb, standing, with cornet, starred in the 1955 movie **Pete Kelly's Blues.**

Benny Goodman recorded the soundtrack for the 1955 film *The Benny Goodman Story*, starring Steve Allen. Sal Mineo played a troubled Gene Krupa in the 1959 *Gene Krupa Story*. Sticking strictly to what he knew best—writing music—Duke Ellington penned the score for *Anatomy of a Murder* in 1959, the same year that Danny Kaye played bandleader Red Nichols in *The Five Pennies*, an emotional movie that featured music by Nichols, Bob Crosby, and Louis Armstrong. Singer Ella Fitzgerald was featured in *Pete Kelly's Blues*, a 1956 movie about jazz musicians becoming involved with gangsters in the 1920s. And the erratic and controversial life of Billie Holiday was the subject of the 1972 film *Lady Sings the Blues*, starring Diana Ross.

New," "Blue Boogie," "Cool World," and "Cool Breeze." By 1939, Gillespie had joined Cab Calloway's band in New York, and had begun to make slight changes in the arrangements he wrote for the group; these changes signaled the advent of a new style that would come to be known as "bebop" or "bop" and would change the face of jazz forever.

There is much speculation about who actually formulated bebop out of the Swing style, but there is little doubt that the music came out of clubs where musicians gathered, such as Minton's Playhouse in Harlem. Many of the musicians who hung out there at the end of the decade have at one time been given

The new style of jazz first became evident when Charlie Parker toured with Billy Eckstine in 1944.

credit for changing the direction of the commercial music of the time by making it cleaner, sharper, and more succinct, and finally adding the musical interval known as the flatted fifth: alto saxophonist Charlie Parker, Dizzy Gillespie, guitarist Charlie Christian, pianists Earl Hines and Thelonius Monk (1920–1985). Musicologists argue over their motivation: Was it that they sensed the end of the commercial success of Swing, or was it a search for different, more innovative music? No doubt each player had his own motivations, and resulted in a transition that built the foundation for what would follow in the world of modern jazz.

Recommended Listening

Louis Armstrong
"I Got Rhythm" (written by George Gershwin, recorded 1930)

"Star Dust" (written by Hoagy Carmichael, 1929; recorded 1931)

"Brother Bill" (Louis Armstrong, 1942)

"Ain't Misbehavin'" (written by Fats Waller, 1929)

"Falling in Love with You" (written by Joseph Meyer, 1926)

Count Basie
"Shoe Shine Boy" (written by Saul Chaplin and Sammy Cahn, 1936)

"Oh, Lady Be Good" (written by George Gershwin and Ira Gershwin, 1924)

"One O'Clock Jump" (written by Count Basie and Harry James, 1938)

"Our Love Was Meant to Be" (arranged by Skip Martin, 1937)

Bix Beiderbecke
"In a Mist" (Bix Beiderbecke, 1928)

"I'm Coming Virginia" (written by Donald Heywood and Will Marion Cook, 1926)

Cab Calloway
"I've Got the World on a String" (written by Ted Koehler and Harold Arlen, 1932)

"Bugle Call Rag" (written by Jack Pettis, Billy Meyers, and Elmer Schoebel, 1923)

"Minnie the Moocher" (written by Cab Calloway, Irving Mills, and Clarence Gaskill, 1931)

"Somebody Stole My Gal" (written by Leo Wood, 1918; recorded 1931)

"I Gotta Right to Sing the Blues" (written by Ted Koehler and Harold Arlen, 1932)

Jimmy Dorsey
"Stompin' at the Savoy" (written by Benny Goodman, Edgar Sampson, Chick Webb, and Andy Razaf, 1936; recorded 1939)

"Don't Be That Way" (written by Mitchell Parish, Benny Goodman, and Edgar Sampson, 1938; recorded 1939)

"Tangerine" (written by Johnny Mercer and Victor Schertzinger, 1942)

Tommy Dorsey
"I'm Getting Sentimental Over You" (written by George Bassman and Ned Washington, 1932)

"Say It" (written by Jimmy McHugh and Frank Loesser, 1940)

"Annie Laurie" (written by Alicia Ann Spottiswoode, 1838; recorded 1938)

Duke Ellington
"It Don't Mean a Thing if It Ain't Got That Swing" (Duke Ellington, 1932)

"Ain't Misbehavin'" (written by Fats Waller, 1933)

"Don't Get Around Much Anymore" (Duke Ellington, 1940)

"Solitude" (Duke Ellington, 1934)

Benny Goodman
"King Porter Stomp" (written by Jelly Roll Morton, 1924; arranged by Fletcher Henderson, 1935)

"Stompin' at the Savoy" (written by Benny Goodman, Edgar Sampson, Chick Webb, and Andy Razaf, 1936)

"Blue Moon" (written by Lorenz Hart and Richard Rodgers, 1934)

"Basin Street Blues" (written by Spencer Williams, 1929; recorded 1935)

Lionel Hampton
"Hamp's Boogie Woogie" (Lionel Hampton, 1940)

"Muskrat Ramble" (written by Edward "Kid" Ory and Ray Gilbert, 1926)

"I Can't Get Started" (written by Ira Gershwin and Vernon Duke, 1935)

"I'd Be Lost Without You" (written by Walter Donaldson, Bob Wright, and Chet Forrest, 1937)

Coleman Hawkins
"Honeysuckle Rose" (written by Fats Waller and Andy Razaf, 1929)

"If I Could Be With You One Hour Tonight" (written by Henry Creamer and Jimmy P. Johnson, 1926)

Woody Herman
"Caldonia" (written by Fleecie Moore, 1946)

"The Music Stopped" (written by Jimmy McHugh and Harold Adamson, 1944)

"Summer Sequence" (written by Ralph Burns, 1946)

Fletcher Henderson
"Christopher Columbus" (written by Chu Berry, 1936; arranged by Horace Henderson)

"Jangled Nerves" (written by Fletcher Henderson and Roger Moore, 1936)

Earl "Fatha" Hines

"Bubbling Over" (arranged by Lawrence Dixon, 1933)

"Rosetta" (written by Earl Hines and Henri Wood, 1933)

Harry James

"Ciribiribin" (written by Rudolf Thaler and Alberto Pestalozza, 1898; recorded 1943)

"All or Nothing at All" (written by Jack Lawrence and Arthur Altman, 1940)

Gene Krupa

"After You've Gone" (written by Henry Creamer and Turner Layton, 1918)

"Rockin' Chair" (written by Hoagy Carmichael, 1930)

"Leave Us Leap" (written by Eddie Finckel, 1944)

"Opus One" (written by Sy Oliver, 1944)

"Boogie Blues" (written by Sy Oliver, 1945)

Jimmie Lunceford

"White Heat" (written by Will Hudson, 1934)

"Jazznocracy" (written by Will Hudson, 1934)

"Swingin' Uptown" (written by Sy Oliver, 1934)

"Rose Room" (written by Art Hickman and Harry Williams, 1917)

"Mood Indigo" (written by Duke Ellington, Irving Mills, and Barney Bigard, 1931)

"Stratosphere" (Jimmie Lunceford, 1934)

Glenn Miller

"Chattanooga Choo-Choo" (written by Mack Gordon and Harry Warren, 1940)

"In the Mood" (written by Joe Garland, 1930; recorded 1939)

"Pennsylvania 6-5000" (written and arranged by Jerry Gray, 1939)

"Time On My Hands" (written by Vincent Youmans, 1930)

"Moonlight Serenade" (Glenn Miller, 1939)

"Wham Re-Bop-Boom-Bam" (written by Eddie Durham, 1939)

"Juke Box Saturday Night" (written by Paul McGrane and Al Stillman, 1942)

Red Norvo (with Mildred Bailey)

"Remember" (written by Irving Berlin, 1942)

"Smoke Dreams" (written by Eddie Sauter, 1937)

Artie Shaw

"Blue Skies" (written by Irving Berlin, 1925)

"Begin the Beguine" (written by Cole Porter, 1935)

Art Tatum

"Tea for Two" (written by Vincent Youmans, 1933)

"Gone with the Wind" (written by Herbert Magidson and Allie Wrubel, 1937)

"Stormy Weather" (written by Harold Arlen and Ted Koehler, 1937)

"Over the Rainbow" (written by Harold Arlen and E.Y. Harburg, 1939)

Jack Teagarden

"I Gotta Right to Sing the Blues" (written by Ted Koehler and Harold Arlen, 1932)

"The Sheik of Araby" (written by Ted Snyder, 1921)

"Basin Street Blues" (written by Spencer Williams, 1929)

Chick Webb

"Heebie Jeebies" (written by Louis Armstrong, 1926; arranged by Benny Carter, 1931)

"Let's Get Together" (written by Edgar Sampson, 1931)

"Soft and Sweet" (written by Edgar Sampson, 1931)

"That Naughty Waltz" (written by Sol P. Levy and Edwin Stanley, 1919; recorded 1936)

"Squeeze Me" (written by Fats Waller, 1925; recorded 1936)

Teddy Wilson

"Smoke Gets in Your Eyes" (written by Jerome Kern, 1933; recorded 1941)

"After You've Gone" (written by Harry Creamer and Turner Layton, 1918; recorded 1935)

"Sailin'" (Teddy Wilson, 1935)

"Body & Soul" (written by John Green, Edward Heyman, Robert Sour, and Frank Eyton, 1930)

"Downhearted Blues" (written by Alberta Hunter, 1923)

Recommended Reading

Berendt, Joachim E. *The Jazz Book, From Ragtime to Fusion and Beyond*. Brooklyn, N.Y.: Lawrence Hill Books, 1992.

Brask, Ole, photographs; Morgenstern, Dan, text. *Jazz People*. New York: Harry N. Abrams, Inc., 1976.

Collier, James Lincoln. *Duke Ellington*. New York: Macmillan, 1991.

Delannoy, Luc. Elena B. Olio, trans. *Pres: The Story of Lester Young*. Fayetteville, Ark.: The University of Arkansas Press, 1993.

Feather, Leonard. *The Encyclopedia of Jazz*. New York: Da Capo Press, 1960.

Fernett, Gene. *Swing Out: Great Negro Dance Bands*. New York: Da Capo Press, 1993.

Firestone, Ross. *Swing, Swing, Swing: The Life & Times of Benny Goodman*. New York: W.W. Norton & Company, 1993.

Giddins, Gary. *Satchmo*. New York: Anchor Books/Doubleday, 1988.

Gridley, Mark C. *Jazz Styles: History and Analysis*. 4th ed. Old Tappan, N.J.: Prentice Hall, 1990.

Lyons, Len, and Don Perlo. *Jazz Portraits: The Lives and Music of the Jazz Masters*. New York: Quill, 1989.

McCarthy, Andrew. *Big Band Jazz*. New York: G.P. Putnam's Sons, 1974.

Meltzer, David, ed. *Reading Jazz*. San Francisco: Mercury House, 1993.

Rattenbury, Ken. *Duke Ellington, Jazz Composer*. New Haven, Conn.: Yale University Press, 1990.

Schuller, Gunther. *The Swing Era: The Development of Jazz, 1930–1945*. New York: Oxford University Press, 1989.

Walker, Leo. *The Big Band Almanac*. New York: Da Capo Press, 1989.

Photography Credits

Front and back cover, and compact disc: Photofest
Endpapers: Archive Photos
Archive Photos: 55
Archive Photos/Frank Driggs Collection: 44, 51
Frank Driggs Collection: 2, 9, 11, 14, 15, 16, 17, 18, 32, 34, 35, 36, 38, 41 43, 45, 46, 48, 49, 53, 57, 58
FPG International: 42
Lester Glassner Collection/Neal Peters: 10, 24, 25, 30, 31, 40, 50, 54
©William P. Gottlieb/Retna Ltd.: 59
Max Jones/©Redferns/ Retna Ltd.: 12, 37
Neal Peters Collection: 6, 26
Ray Avery's Jazz Archives: 20, 52, 56
Stock Montage, Inc., Chicago, IL: 13
Bob Willoughby/©Redferns/Retna Ltd.: 22
Courtesy of Sony Music Entertainment, Inc.: 29

Index